ABC

in

Los Angeles

and LA County

All 'Bout Cities

Murray Hill Books LLC

www.murrayhillbooks.com

Aa

apartment
building
el edificio de apartamentos

ambulances
las ambulancias

Angelino Heights

avocados
los
aguacates

Bb

bicycles
las bicicletas

birds
los
pájaros

basketball
game
un juego de
baloncesto

bus stop
la parada
de
autobús

buses
los
autobuses

Cc

churro
un churro

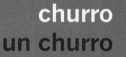

car wash
un túnel
de lavado

Caltrans building
el edificio Caltrans

cat
el gato

Chinatown
el barrio chino

**canyon
and coast**
el cañón y la costa

Coliseum
el Coliseo

City Hall
el ayuntamiento

Dd

Disney Hall
el salón Disney

dim sum

dogs
los perros

Dorothy Chandler Pavilion
el Pabellón Dorothy Chandler

Dodger Stadium
el Dodger Stadium

dumpster
un contenedor de basura

E e

Echo Park
el Parque Echo

escalator
la escalera
mecánica

elevator
el ascensor

Ff

fresh fruit
la frutas frescas

fruit vendor
el vendedor de frutas

farmers market
el mercado agrícola

fire engine
un coche de bomberos

fire
hydrant
la boca
de incendio

fishermen
los pescadores

flags
las banderas

Gg

Grand Central Market   el Gran Mercado Central

**gas station
la gasolinera**

Getty Museum   el Museo Getty

Hh

graffiti
un graffiti

hot dog vendor
el vendedor
de perros calientes

**houses
on a hill**
unas casas
sobre
una loma

Hollywood sign
el letrero Hollywood

Ii

intersection
el cruce

ice cream
un helado

ice cream vendors
los vendedores de helado

Jj

joggers
los corredores

Japanese Village Plaza
la Plaza del Barrio Japonés

Kk

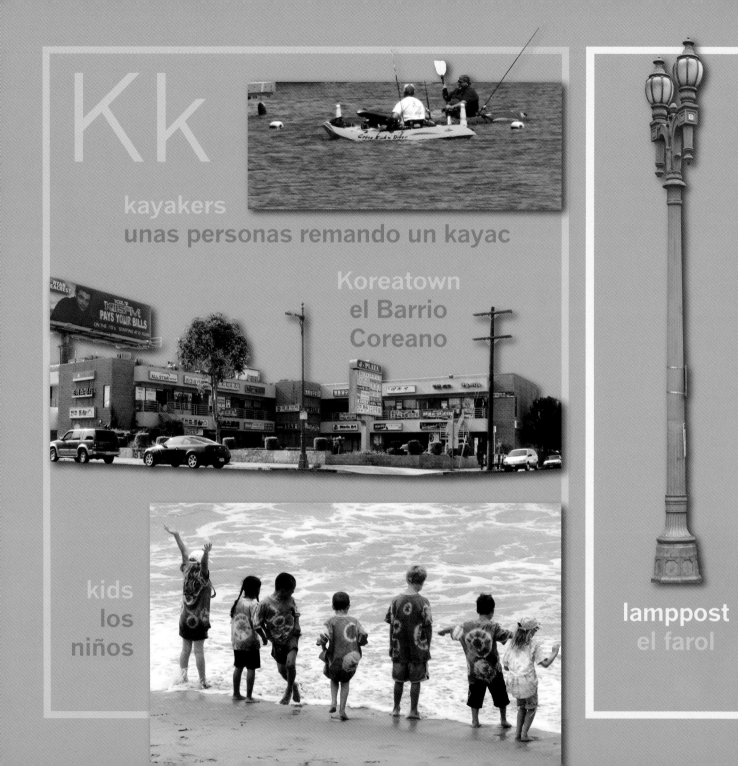

kayakers
unas personas remando un kayac

Koreatown
el Barrio
Coreano

kids
los
niños

lamppost
el farol

L l

Lakers fans
los fans de
los Lakers

license plate
una matrícula

lighthouse
el faro

lifeguard station
el puesto de
salvavidas

MAR California 2009
R 3087413
6CUV915

Mm

mailbox
el buzón

musician
el músico

meters
los
parquímetros

murals
los
murales

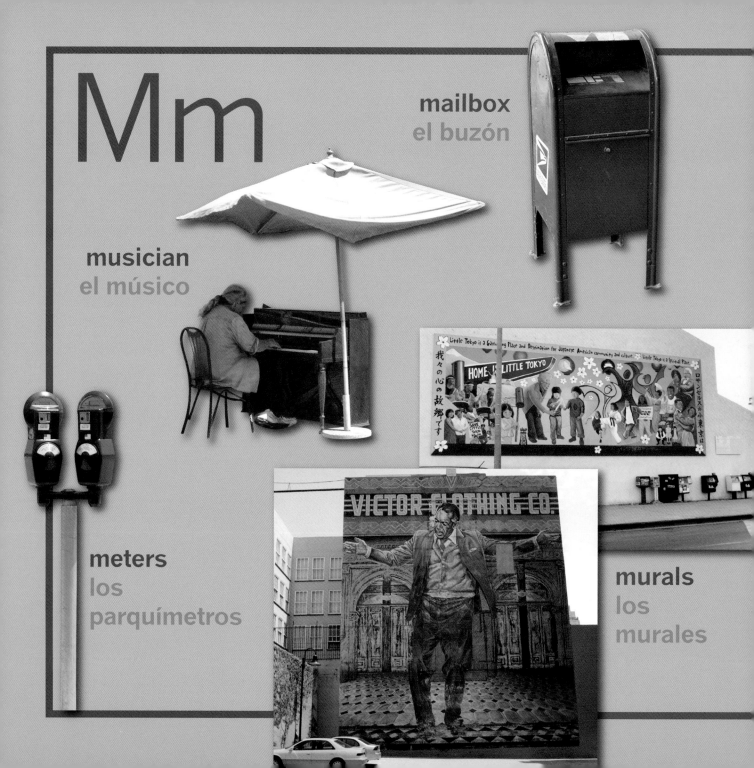

mail carrier
el cartero

map book
el libro de mapas

Muscle Beach
la Playa Muscle

Mulholland Drive
el Paseo Mulholland

manhole cover
la tapa de la alcantarilla

Nn

nachos
los nachos

newspaper
el periódico

newsstand
el kiosco de
periódicos

newspaper boxes
las cajas de periódicos

Oo

observatory
el observatorio

overpass
el paso elevado

orator
el orador

oil pumps
las bombas
de petróleo

oranges
las
naranjas

Broken
Promises

Pp

Pacific coast
la costa Pacifica

parking structure
el estacionamiento

police officer
el policía

palm trees
las
palmeras

pay phone
el teléfono público

patrol car
el coche patrulla

pigeons and
picnic table
las palomas
y una mesa
de comida
campestre

Pershing Square
la Plaza Pershing

port
el puerto

Qq

quesadilla
la quesadilla

The Queen Mary
el Queen Mary

regulations
el reglamento

NO

DOGS ON
BIKE PATH

WELCOME
TO THE BEACH

ARROWHEAD

Rr

recycling
el bote de reciclaje

rose garden
el jardín de rosas

**Rodeo
Drive
el Paseo
Rodeo**

**rollerbladers
los patinadores**

Ss

school buses
los autobuses de transporte escolar

skateboarder
el patineto

sand, surf, seaweed
la arena, las olas, la alga marina

Santa Monica pier
el embarcadero de Santa Monica

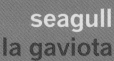

seagull
la gaviota

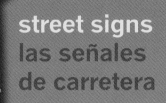

street signs
las señales
de carretera

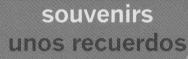

souvenirs
unos recuerdos

speed limit
la velocidad
máxima

sunglasses
las gafas de sol

salads
las ensaladas

Tt

traffic
el tráfico

trash cans
los cubos
de basura

tamale
un tamale

taxis
los taxis

tar pits
las canteras de alquitrán

traffic light
el semáforo

tourists
los turistas

Uu

**umbrellas
las
sombrillas**

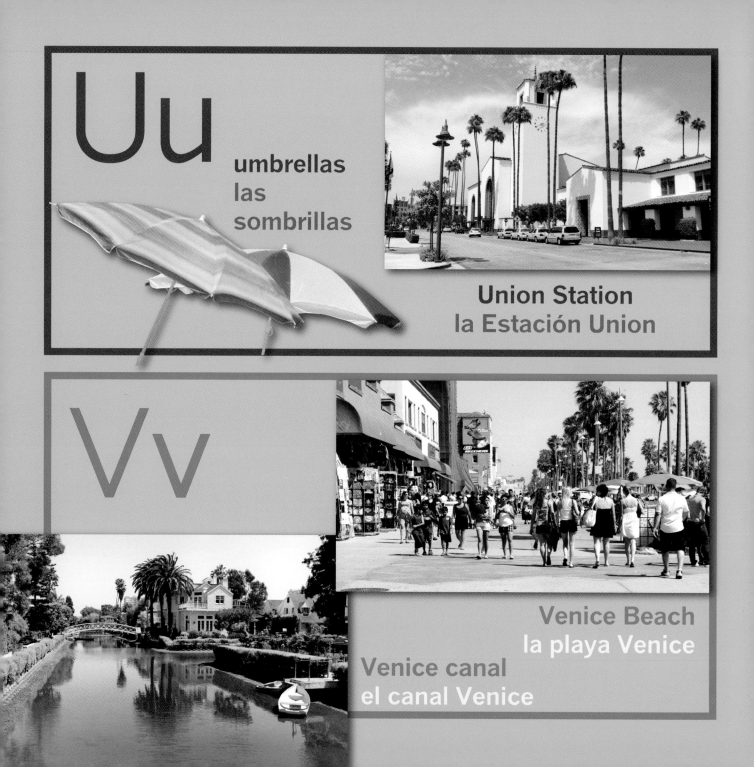

**Union Station
la Estación Union**

Vv

**Venice Beach
la playa Venice**

**Venice canal
el canal Venice**

Ww

Watts Towers
las Torres Watts

water fountain
el bebedero

walk signal
la señal de caminar

Wilshire Boulevard
el Bulevar Wilshire

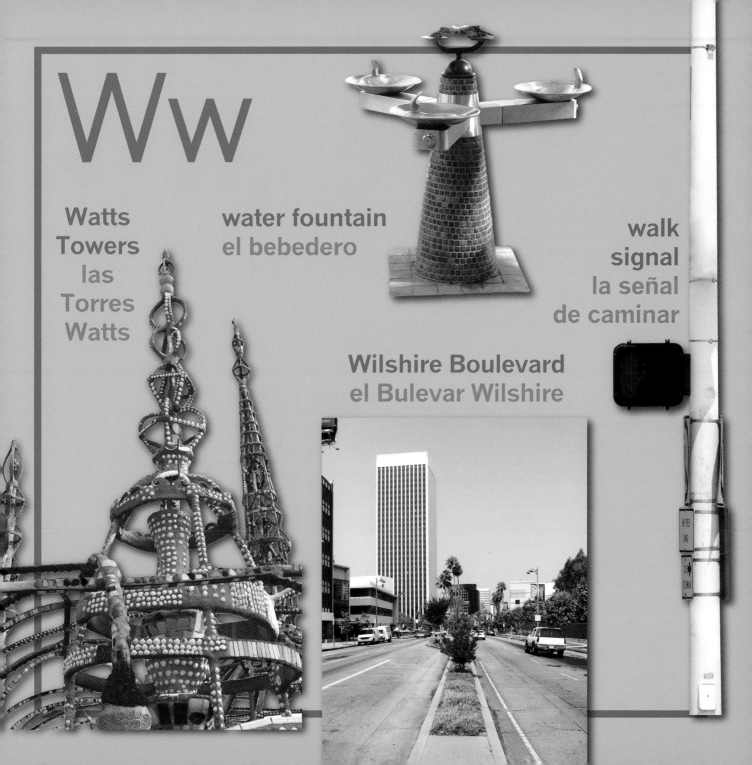

Xx

xing
(crossing)
**el cruce
de peatones**

**Ximeno Avenue
la avenida
Ximeno**

Yy

**yachts
los yates**

Zz

Zuma Beach
la Playa Zuma

Murray Hill Books, LLC
P.O. Box 4393
New York, NY 10163

www.murrayhillbooks.com
info@murrayhillbooks.com
SAN 256-3622

Library of Congress Control Number: 2008941339
ISBN: 9781935139027

Design and Editing by Robin Segal.
Additional photographic editing by Miriam Margulies and Andrew Lim.

Translation by Jean-Pierre Fournier.

"All 'Bout Cities" is a Registered Trademark.

Look for more "All 'Bout Cities" titles at:

www.allboutcities.com